HANDPICKED TO SERVE #THEKING

PREPARING TODAY'S YOUTH TO BE TOMORROW'S LEADERS

JOHN BRITTON

HANDPICKED TO SERVE #THEKING

Copyright © 2016 by John Britton
All rights reserved.

Published by:
NyreePress Literary Group
Fort Worth, TX 76161
1-800-972-3864
www.nyreepress.com

All rights reserved. No part of this book may be used or reproduced by any means, graphic, electronic, or mechanical, including photocopying, recording, taping or by any information storage retrieval system without the written permission of the publisher. Copying this book is both illegal and unethical.

Scripture quotations are taken from the Holy Bible, New Living Translation, copyright ©1996, 2004, 2007, 2013, 2015 by Tyndale House Foundation. Used by permission of Tyndale House Publishers, Inc., Carol Stream, Illinois 60188. All rights reserved.

ISBN print: 978-0-9972921-8-3

Library of Congress Control Number: pending
Christian Living / Youth
Printed in the United States of America

Contents

How to think calmly and make wise decisions 1

How to choose between good and bad advice 5

How to be humble 9

When to stand up for what they believe in 13

How to draw strength from God 17

How to do what's right at all times 21

When to accept help out of a bad situation 25

How to take the initiative 29

How to give people what they need 33

How to be a servant leader 37

How to grow in favor with God and man 41

That they're already equipped for the job 45

Acknowledgment

First and foremost, I would like to thank God for producing a workbook through me that will prayerfully have an impact on those that read it and honestly address the reflection questions. Believe me when I say that all things are possible when Christ is on your side.

I'd like to dedicate my first book to the memory of my mother, Myra Britton, and grandmother, Nancy Heath, two of the greatest influences in my life. Also, I would like to thank my beautiful wife, Eboni, my sons John Jr and Justin, my natural and spiritual family and friends for their support and encouragement in this endeavor.

I pray that this book will bless the reader like it blessed the writer.

To God be the Glory!

John

A GOOD LEADER KNOWS...

How to think calmly and make wise decisions

A fool gives full vent to anger, but a wise person quietly holds it back. – Proverbs 29:11

Lesson Text: Acts 5: 27 – 40

²⁷ Then they brought the apostles before the high council, where the high priest confronted them. ²⁸ "We gave you strict orders never again to teach in this man's name!" he said. "Instead, you have filled all Jerusalem with your teaching about him, and you want to make us responsible for his death!" ²⁹ But Peter and the apostles replied, "We must obey God rather than any human authority. ³⁰ The God of our ancestors raised Jesus from the dead after you killed him by hanging him on a cross. ³¹ Then God put him in the place of honor at his right hand as Prince and Savior. He did this so the people of Israel would repent of their sins and be forgiven. ³² We are witnesses of these things and so is the Holy Spirit, who is given by God to those who obey him." ³³ When they heard this, the high council was furious and decided to kill them.

³⁴ But one member, a Pharisee named Gamaliel, who was an expert in religious law and respected by all the people, stood up

and ordered that the men be sent outside the council chamber for a while. ³⁵ Then he said to his colleagues, "Men of Israel, take care what you are planning to do to these men! ³⁶ Some time ago there was that fellow Theudas, who pretended to be someone great. About 400 others joined him, but he was killed, and all his followers went their various ways. The whole movement came to nothing. ³⁷ After him, at the time of the census, there was Judas of Galilee. He got people to follow him, but he was killed, too, and all his followers were scattered.

³⁸ "So my advice is, leave these men alone. Let them go. If they are planning and doing these things merely on their own, it will soon be overthrown. ³⁹ But if it is from God, you will not be able to overthrow them. You may even find yourselves fighting against God!" ⁴⁰ The others accepted his advice. They called in the apostles and had them flogged. Then they ordered them never again to speak in the name of Jesus, and they let them go.

Points to Ponder (P2P) Then:

- The Apostles disobeyed the commands of the High Priest and religious leaders, who instructed them to not teach in the name of Jesus. They decided that it was better to obey God than man.

- The religious leaders were upset and wanted to kill the Apostles because they didn't obey them and also accused them of killing Jesus.

- Gamaliel had the Apostles removed from the room and suggested that the other leaders think about what they were about to do and consider the consequences.

_____

_____

P2P Now:

- There are going to be situations in which we are going to have to either do what our friends say or obey God. As Christians, we are to obey and trust God even though it may get us in trouble with our friends.

- Sometimes people are going to want to hurt us, talk about us, or be mean to us simply because we are trying to do the right thing instead of doing what they want us to do.

- There are times when we will have to remove ourselves from situations, check our emotions, and think about the good or bad outcome from our decisions.

_____

_____

Real Talk:

Can you think of a time or situation in which you or someone else did something before they thought about it? What are some of the consequences from doing this?

Life Lessons:

(1) Think before you act.

(2) Keep your emotions in check.

(3) Don't be afraid to do what's right.

#WhatIlearned:

_____

_____

_____

_____

_____

_____

A GOOD LEADER KNOWS...

How to choose between good and bad advice

Hmmm, who should I listen to?

Lesson Text: 1 Kings 12: 4 – 14

⁴ "Your father was a hard master," they said. "Lighten the harsh labor demands and heavy taxes that your father imposed on us. Then we will be your loyal subjects." ⁵ Rehoboam replied, "Give me three days to think this over. Then come back for my answer." So the people went away.

⁶ Then King Rehoboam discussed the matter with the older men who had counseled his father, Solomon. "What is your advice?" he asked. "How should I answer these people?" ⁷ The older counselors replied, "If you are willing to be a servant to these people today and give them a favorable answer, they will always be your loyal subjects."

⁸ But Rehoboam rejected the advice of the older men and instead asked the opinion of the young men who had grown up with him and were now his advisers. ⁹ "What is your advice?" he asked them.

"How should I answer these people who want me to lighten the burdens imposed by my father?"

[10] The young men replied, "This is what you should tell those complainers who want a lighter burden: 'My little finger is thicker than my father's waist! [11] Yes, my father laid heavy burdens on you, but I'm going to make them even heavier! My father beat you with whips, but I will beat you with scorpions!'"

[12] Three days later Jeroboam and all the people returned to hear Rehoboam's decision, just as the king had ordered. [13] But Rehoboam spoke harshly to the people, for he rejected the advice of the older counselors [14] and followed the counsel of his younger advisers. He told the people, "My father laid heavy burdens on you, but I'm going to make them even heavier! My father beat you with whips, but I will beat you with scorpions!"

P2P Then:

- Rehoboam was made king and the people asked him how he was going to rule over them. So, he sought advice from the older men and his childhood friends to help him decide. (1 Kings 12: 1-3)

- The older men told him to be a servant to the people, serve them, answer them, and speak good words to them. The people would then serve him forever. His childhood friends told him to work the people harder, and punish them more than his father, Solomon, did.

- Rehoboam went with the advice of his childhood friends, and this decision caused the twelve tribes to go from one united nation to two divided kingdoms. (1 Kings 12: 16-20)

P2P Now:

- As up and coming leaders, we are going to have to make some tough decisions. If time permits, it's a good practice to seek advice from others. Others could be our parents, spouses, godly people, siblings, teachers, friends, or sometimes people we dislike. Most of the time, it's better to heed the advice from older and more experienced people.

- Good leaders evaluate the advice that is given and make decisions based on the best interest of those we lead, as opposed to what will only benefit us. Good leaders put others' needs above their own.

- When considering advice, we have to make sure that we consider the consequences of our decisions that we sought advice for. Will our decision make things better or worse? Make sure that following the advice given lines up with biblical principles.

Real Talk:

What if Rehoboam had followed the advice of the older, wiser men? What do you think the outcome would have been? What can happen to us today if we follow bad advice?

Life Lessons:

(1) Not all advice is good advice.

(2) Consider the source and motives of those we receive advice from.

(3) Although we may receive advice, we are responsible for our own decisions.

#WhatIlearned

_____

_____

_____

_____

_____

A GOOD LEADER KNOWS...

How to be humble

I'm a beast and you're nothing!

Lesson Text: Luke 18: 9-14

⁹ Then Jesus told this story to some who had great confidence in their own righteousness and scorned everyone else: ¹⁰ "Two men went to the Temple to pray. One was a Pharisee, and the other was a despised tax collector. ¹¹ The Pharisee stood by himself and prayed this prayer: 'I thank you, God, that I am not like other people—cheaters, sinners, adulterers. I'm certainly not like that tax collector! ¹² I fast twice a week, and I give you a tenth of my income.'

¹³ "But the tax collector stood at a distance and dared not even lift his eyes to heaven as he prayed. Instead, he beat his chest in sorrow, saying, 'O God, be merciful to me, for I am a sinner.' ¹⁴ I tell you, this sinner, not the Pharisee, returned home justified before God. For those who exalt themselves will be humbled, and those who humble themselves will be exalted."

P2P Then:

- Jesus was talking to those who looked down on others and thought that they were better than them.

- The Pharisee was bragging about himself and putting down others, including the dishonest tax collector.

- In God's eyes, the dishonest tax collector's prayer and view of himself was better than the Pharisees'.

_____

_____

P2P Now:

- A good leader should be: sincerely humble, not proud or arrogant, free from pride, and they should not think they are better than others.

- Humility is not being weak, soft, or a push-over. Christ made it a cornerstone of Christian character.

- You can either humble yourself, or God will humble you (Luke 14:11). God humbles us to bring us into obedience.

_____

_____

Real Talk:

Give an example of someone who thought that they were all that, and got embarrassed. Was it you?

Life Lessons:

(1) Humility is power under control.

(2) Put others before yourself.

(3) You can be humble and still be a strong effective leader.

(4) Being humble does not mean letting people walk all over you.

#WhatIlearned

_____

_____

_____

_____

_____

_____

_____

A GOOD LEADER KNOWS...

When to stand up for what they believe in

Elijah vs. the false Prophets

Lesson Text: 1 Kings 18: 16-24

[16] So Obadiah went to tell Ahab that Elijah had come, and Ahab went out to meet Elijah. [17] When Ahab saw him, he exclaimed, "So, is it really you, you troublemaker of Israel?"

[18] "I have made no trouble for Israel," Elijah replied. "You and your family are the troublemakers, for you have refused to obey the commands of the LORD and have worshiped the images of Baal instead.[19] Now summon all Israel to join me at Mount Carmel, along with the 450 prophets of Baal and the 400 prophets of Asherah who are supported by Jezebel."

[20] So Ahab summoned all the people of Israel and the prophets to Mount Carmel. [21] Then Elijah stood in front of them and said, "How much longer will you waver, hobbling between two opinions? If the LORD is God, follow him! But if Baal is God, then follow him!" But the people were completely silent.

[22] Then Elijah said to them, "I am the only prophet of the LORD who is left, but Baal has 450 prophets. [23] Now bring two bulls.

The prophets of Baal may choose whichever one they wish and cut it into pieces and lay it on the wood of their altar, but without setting fire to it. I will prepare the other bull and lay it on the wood on the altar, but not set fire to it.[24] Then call on the name of your god, and I will call on the name of the LORD. The god who answers by setting fire to the wood is the true God!" And all the people agreed.

P2P Then:

- Because Elijah stood firm in his beliefs, King Ahab called him a trouble maker.

- Elijah believed and trusted God so much that he challenged the prophets to a contest in which he firmly believed that he would win because he had God on his side.

- The false prophets stood firm in their beliefs as well; they accepted the challenge. They called and cried out to Baal from morning to evening. They danced around the alter, and even cut themselves with knives and swords to get an answer from him. In the end, they died for what they believed in.

_____

_____

P2P Now:

- As leaders sometimes we are going to have to take a stand against something that we don't believe in, or take a stand for something we *do* believe in. (1 Kings 18:21).

- It may seem like we're all alone when we stand up for what we believe in, but in fact, we're not alone. Our decision to take a stand may encourage others to join us.

- Standing up for what we believe in may not always be comfortable for us, and there may be a risk involved. But, if you truly believe it, it's worth the risk.

_____

_____

Real Talk:

Can you think of a time when you or someone you know stood up for what they believed? What was the outcome?

Life Lessons:

(1) Stand up for what you believe in, even if you stand alone.

(2) Everyone is not always going to agree with you.

(3) It takes courage, strength, and a strong will to stand up for what you believe.

HANDPICKED TO SERVE

#WhatIlearned

_____

_____

_____

_____

_____

_____

A GOOD LEADER KNOWS...

How to draw strength from God

You're the leader, so it's your fault.

Lesson Text: 1 Samuel 30: 1 – 6

Three days later, when David and his men arrived home at their town of Ziklag, they found that the Amalekites had made a raid into the Negev and Ziklag; they had crushed Ziklag and burned it to the ground. [2] They had carried off the women and children and everyone else but without killing anyone.

[3] When David and his men saw the ruins and realized what had happened to their families, [4] they wept until they could weep no more. [5] David's two wives, Ahinoam from Jezreel and Abigail, the widow of Nabal from Carmel, were among those captured. [6] David was now in great danger because all his men were very bitter about losing their sons and daughters, and they began to talk of stoning him. But David found strength in the LORD his God.

P2P Then:

- David was favored by God, was destined to be the next king, and was a mighty warrior. Yet, his hometown was

- raided and burned to the ground. All the women and children were taken captive.

- They all mourned together, but afterwards, David's men quickly turned on him. They wanted to stone him because they felt that he was to blame for the loss of their families.

- Instead of waiting on someone to defend him or give him a pep talk, David encouraged himself in the Lord his God. In other words, he turned to God for hope, courage, confidence, and guidance.

_____

_____

P2P Now:

- There are going to be times when we feel like we are on top of the world. Things will go well for us and we will be good Christians. It will all seem like life is perfect and then suddenly, something will go wrong.

- When we're the leader and things start to go wrong, people will look for someone to blame; even if it isn't entirely their fault. As a leader we have to be prepared to deal with these types of situations.

- When no one else believes in us and it seems like everyone is turning on us, we have to remember who to turn to in a time of crisis. God is our strength, our rock, our fortress, and our savior. He is our shield, the power that saves us, and our place of safety.

_____

_____

Real Talk:

Give an example of a time when you felt like everyone was against you and you had to encourage yourself by turning to God or by giving yourself a pep talk. If you can't think of a time, think of someone who stood alone on something and came out victorious.

Life Lessons:

(1) Sometimes God will allow bad things to happen to us.

(2) We have to look for a solution rather than someone to blame.

(3) People will be your friend one minute and your enemy the next.

#WhatIlearned:

_____

_____

_____

_____

A GOOD LEADER KNOWS...

How to do what's right at all times

So whoever knows the right thing to do and fails to do it, for him it is sin. (James 4:17) ESV

Lesson Text: : 1 Samuels 24: 1 – 7

After Saul returned from fighting the Philistines, he was told that David had gone into the wilderness of En-gedi. ² So Saul chose 3,000 elite troops from all Israel and went to search for David and his men near the rocks of the wild goats.

³ At the place where the road passes some sheepfolds, Saul went into a cave to relieve himself. But as it happened, David and his men were hiding farther back in that very cave!

⁴ "Now's your opportunity!" David's men whispered to him. "Today the Lord is telling you, 'I will certainly put your enemy into your power, to do with as you wish.'" So David crept forward and cut off a piece of the hem of Saul's robe.

⁵ But then David's conscience began bothering him because he had cut Saul's robe. ⁶ He said to his men, "The LORD forbid that I should do this to my lord the king. I shouldn't attack the LORD's

anointed one, for the Lord himself has chosen him." [7] So David restrained his men and did not let them kill Saul.

P2P Then:

- Saul was already the king, so why did he waste time, energy and resources to try and kill David?

- David's men tried to convince him to kill Saul while he was alone in the cave where they were hiding. They didn't see anything wrong with killing Saul because of the way he treated David.

- David cut off a piece of Saul's robe and immediately felt remorseful. He knew that he should not have touched Saul at all. Why?

_____

_____

P2P Now:

- If God made you the leader, why would you worry about or feel threatened by other folks in your group or organization? The right thing to do is to help them advance instead of hurting them.

- God will never tell you or tempt you to do bad things; these are choices that we make. We have to know what "right" feels like.

- We can't let our friends or those we lead talk us into doing something bad. We have to do what's right at all times.

___

___

Real Talk:

Have you ever done something bad and immediately regretted it? What was it that caused you to feel remorseful?

Life Lessons:

(1) When our friends or a situation are pressuring us, we have to choose to do the right thing.

(2) If you make a bad choice, be confident and brave enough to admit your mistake and fix it.

(3) Sometimes our decision to do good will influence those around us to do good.

(4) We have to resist the temptation to do something bad in order to benefit ourselves.

HANDPICKED TO SERVE

#WhatIlearned:

_____

_____

_____

_____

_____

_____

_____

A GOOD LEADER KNOWS...

When to accept help out of a bad situation

Run Lot Run.

Lesson Text: Genesis 19: 12 – 17

¹² Meanwhile, the angels questioned Lot. "Do you have any other relatives here in the city?" they asked. "Get them out of this place—your sons-in-law, sons, daughters, or anyone else. ¹³ For we are about to destroy this city completely. The outcry against this place is so great it has reached the LORD, and he has sent us to destroy it."

¹⁴ So Lot rushed out to tell his daughters' fiancés, "Quick, get out of the city! The LORD is about to destroy it." But the young men thought he was only joking.

¹⁵ At dawn the next morning the angels became insistent. "Hurry," they said to Lot. "Take your wife and your two daughters who are here. Get out right now, or you will be swept away in the destruction of the city!"

¹⁶ When Lot still hesitated, the angels seized his hand and the

hands of his wife and two daughters and rushed them to safety outside the city, for the LORD was merciful. ¹⁷ When they were safely out of the city, one of the angels ordered, "Run for your lives! And don't look back or stop anywhere in the valley! Escape to the mountains, or you will be swept away!"

P2P Then:

- Lot asked the old and young men of the city not to do such a wicked thing. He realized that what they wanted to do was wrong and did not agree with it. (Genesis 19:1-11)

- The Angels told Lot to leave or he and his family would be punished for the sins of the city. In other words, they would be punished for other people's sin.

- Lot was hesitant to leave, but he allowed the Angels to lead him out of the city before it was destroyed.

_____

_____

P2P Now:

- We have several options when we realize that we are in a bad situation. We can either:

    (1) choose to stay and willingly be a part of the problem.

(2) ignore it and hope that we don't get caught up in the mess turn to someone to help us get out of the situation.

- If we don't remove ourselves from a bad situation or environment, we may be punished like the ones that are causing the problem. Have you ever heard of guilt by association?

- When God warns us or sends someone to help us out of a bad situation, we have to take advantage of the help.

_____

_____

Real Talk:

Have you ever gotten into trouble just because you were in the wrong place at the wrong time and chose to stay there instead of leaving?

Life Lessons:

(1) Although others are sinning or doing bad things around us, we don't have to do the same.

(2) Sometimes God will use us to help others out of a bad situation. Our job is to reach out and tell them the problem. Ultimately, it is their choice on what they will do.

(3) Once we are out of a bad situation, we can't reflect on or return to what God has delivered us from.

(4) It's ok to accept help from others.

#WhatIlearned:

_____

_____

_____

_____

_____

_____

A GOOD LEADER KNOWS...

How to take the initiative

Can you help me?

Lesson Text: Acts 8:26-39

As for Philip, an angel of the Lord said to him, "Go south down the desert road that runs from Jerusalem to Gaza." [27] So he started out, and he met the treasurer of Ethiopia, a eunuch of great authority under the Kandake, the queen of Ethiopia. The eunuch had gone to Jerusalem to worship, [28] and he was now returning. Seated in his carriage, he was reading aloud from the book of the prophet Isaiah.

[29] The Holy Spirit said to Philip, "Go over and walk along beside the carriage." [30] Philip ran over and heard the man reading from the prophet Isaiah. Philip asked, "Do you understand what you are reading?" [31] The man replied, "How can I, unless someone instructs me?" And he urged Philip to come up into the carriage and sit with him. [32] The passage of Scripture he had been reading was this:"He was led like a sheep to the slaughter. And as a lamb is silent before the shearers, he did not open his mouth. [33] He was humiliated and received no justice.

Who can speak of his descendants? For his life was taken from the earth." ³⁴ The eunuch asked Philip, "Tell me, was the prophet talking about himself or someone else?" ³⁵ So beginning with this same Scripture, Philip told him the Good News about Jesus.

³⁶ As they rode along, they came to some water, and the eunuch said, "Look! There's some water! Why can't I be baptized?"³⁸ He ordered the carriage to stop, and they went down into the water, and Philip baptized him. ³⁹ When they came up out of the water, the Spirit of the Lord snatched Philip away. The eunuch never saw him again but went on his way rejoicing.

P2P Then:

- The Ethiopian Eunuch came all the way from Ethiopia to worship in Jerusalem. He didn't truly understand Christianity, but he committed himself to learning and being a follower.

- He put his pride and insecurities to the side and asked Phillip to help him comprehend the passage of the Bible in which he took the initiative to read aloud and try to understand.

- After Phillip taught him about Jesus, the Ethiopian saw some water and asked to be baptized. He didn't wait for Phillip to ask him if he was ready to go to the next level in his faith.

P2P Now:

- As a leader, sometimes we are going to have to leave our comfort zone in order to learn or experience something new.

- There are times when we'll have to take the initiative to better ourselves. Sometimes that may include asking someone for help. It's not a sign of weakness to ask and accept help from someone.

- Once we learn something new, it's important that we act upon it and try to use it to help ourselves and others who are influenced by our leadership.

_____

_____

Real Talk:

How have you taken the initiative on something in the past? Have you seen someone go get something for themselves and it turned out well? What are some things that you can take the first step on?

Life Lessons:

(1) Without initiative, leaders are simply workers in leadership positions.

(2) Learn how to accept help from people that may be different from us.

(3) We have to look for opportunities and have enough courage to take the first step toward action on some matters.

#WhatIlearned:

_____

_____

_____

_____

_____

_____

A GOOD LEADER KNOWS...

How to give people what they need

You don't need that, what you really need is...

Lesson Text: Acts 3: 1 – 8

Peter and John went to the Temple one afternoon to take part in the three o'clock prayer service. ² As they approached the Temple, a man lame from birth was being carried in. Each day he was put beside the Temple gate, the one called the Beautiful Gate, so he could beg from the people going into the Temple. ³ When he saw Peter and John about to enter, he asked them for some money.

⁴ Peter and John looked at him intently, and Peter said, "Look at us!"⁵ The lame man looked at them eagerly, expecting some money. ⁶ But Peter said, "I don't have any silver or gold for you. But I'll give you what I have. In the name of Jesus Christ the Nazarene, get up and walk!"

⁷ Then Peter took the lame man by the right hand and helped him up. And as he did, the man's feet and ankles were instantly healed and strengthened. ⁸ He jumped up, stood on his feet, and began to walk! Then, walking, leaping, and praising God, he went into the Temple with them.

P2P Then:

- The man was crippled from birth and was not allowed into the Temple because of his disability (2 Samuel 5:8). He could not go into the place that could have given him what he needed.

- Peter realized that the man was asking for the wrong thing. He didn't need a hand-out. He needed strength in his ankle and foot bone to be able to support his weight.

- Peter and John healed him in Jesus' name. They encouraged and helped him use the gift they just gave him.

_____

_____

P2P Now:

- As leaders, we must make sure that we are approachable and open enough where people feel comfortable coming to us for help.

- If you truly want to help someone, give them what they really need and not what they think they need. Don't be afraid to give someone what they need just because it's not what they expected or asked of you.

- People may be surprised, confused, or even upset with us when we give them what they need. We may have to encourage and help them prosper in what they need as opposed to what they want.

_____

_____

Real Talk:

How do you feel when you ask someone (especially a person of authority) for one thing and they give you another? What is an example of when you asked for something but ended up getting something that was better for you than what you had asked?

Life Lessons:

(1) Don't be afraid to give people what they really need. They may not like that you didn't give them what they asked for, but you'll have a clear conscious because you did the right thing.

(2) We can ask God for what we want, but don't be surprised when He gives us what we need instead. If this happens, we should take the time to think about what was given to us and decide if that was what we really needed.

(3) People respect and appreciate leaders who really care about them and show it. Especially when they do what's in their best interest instead of doing it just to please them. What you give them could possibly change their life.

#WhatIlearned:

_____

_____

_____

_____

_____

_____

A GOOD LEADER KNOWS...

How to be a servant leader

No, you first, I insist.

Lesson Text: Luke 22: 24-27

Then they began to argue among themselves about who would be the greatest among them. ²⁵ Jesus told them, "In this world the kings and great men lord it over their people, yet they are called 'friends of the people.' ²⁶ But among you it will be different. Those who are the greatest among you should take the lowest rank, and the leader should be like a servant. ²⁷ Who is more important, the one who sits at the table or the one who serves? The one who sits at the table, of course. But not here! For I am among you as one who serves.

P2P Then:

- The disciples were arguing over which of them would be the greatest disciple after Jesus dies. They were so focused on themselves that they missed what Jesus was trying to tell them.

- Jesus pointed out that the Kings exercised lordship (having authority, control, or power) over the people and the people thought the rulers were helping them and considered them as friends.

- Jesus changed the game. He taught that the greatest among them should be like the least privileged and act as a servant. Jesus was, no doubt, the greatest among them all, and yet He served them. How Jesus treated them may have had a factor in them sticking with Him until the end and beyond.

_____

_____

<u>P2P Now:</u>

- As leaders we can't always be caught up in a struggle about our own personal success, careers or status. We can't be leaders that only serve ourselves and neglect others. It is ok to look after one's self but one's self cannot become more important than others.

- The servant leader has the mindset of servant first, leader second. In other words, they make sure that the needs of others are met before their own. They care about people's lives and not just their own position or job.

- Jesus challenged society's teaching. He taught that greatness came from serving. Sometimes it's hard to humble ourselves to serve others because the world teaches us to be selfish and arrogant when we are the leaders. We are taught to look out for self.

_____

_____

Real Talk:

Would you rather have a leader who is bossy, arrogant and always looking out for themselves, or a leader that really cares about you and takes care of you first?

Life Lessons:

(1) Being a servant keeps us in tune to the needs of others and it keeps us from focusing entirely on ourselves.

(2) If you take care of people, often times they will take care of you. People are happier when good leaders are in charge (Proverbs 29:2).

(3) When you treat people right, they'll stick with you until the end.

HANDPICKED TO SERVE

#WhatIlearned

_____

_____

_____

_____

_____

_____

_____

A GOOD LEADER KNOWS...

How to grow in favor with God and man

And a child shall lead them.

Lesson Text: 1 Samuel 2: 18-26

But Samuel, though he was only a boy, served the LORD. He wore a linen garment like that of a priest.[19] Each year his mother made a small coat for him and brought it to him when she came with her husband for the sacrifice. [20] Before they returned home, Eli would bless Elkanah and his wife and say, "May the LORD give you other children to take the place of this one she gave to the LORD." [21] And the LORD blessed Hannah, and she conceived and gave birth to three sons and two daughters. Meanwhile, Samuel grew up in the presence of the LORD.

[22] Now Eli was very old, but he was aware of what his sons were doing to the people of Israel. He knew, for instance, that his sons were seducing the young women who assisted at the entrance of the Tabernacle.[23] Eli said to them, "I have been hearing reports from all the people about the wicked things you are doing. Why do you keep sinning? [24] You must stop, my sons! The reports I hear among the LORD's people are not good.[25] If someone sins against another person, God can mediate for the guilty party. But if someone sins against the LORD, who can intercede?" But Eli's

sons wouldn't listen to their father, for the LORD was already planning to put them to death. ²⁶ Meanwhile, the boy Samuel grew taller and grew in favor with the LORD and with the people.

P2P Then:

- Samuel was living and working in the church since he was about 3 years old. He was a descendent of the Levitical tribe, so he would have been required to serve in the temple by age 25. (Numbers 8:24-25)

- Although Eli's sons were priests, they were evil and did not have a relationship with God. They took advantage of their positions by corrupting church servants and by cheating and bullying the people who came to offer a sacrifice.

- Although evil things were going on in the Temple, as Samuel grew up, he was considered a good person by God and other people. He didn't do the evil things that were going on around him.

_____

_____

P2P Now:

- As leaders, we have to follow the guidance of others or put ourselves into a position that we can learn about and practice serving God. We are never too young or too old to serve God.

- Not everyone (including church leaders) who are in a positon of authority are good people. Sometimes God allows bad people to be in charge and they take advantage of their position.

- Like Samuel, we have to learn how to live a life that is pleasing to God and be mindful of how we treat people and live before them.

_____

_____

Real Talk:

Have you ever treated someone wrong just because you could? Do you feel like someone is treating you or has treated you wrong just because they could?

Life Lessons:

(1) Getting involved and helping in the church can teach us some valuable life lessons, but our motives must be pure for serving God.

(2) We have to be careful not to get caught up in the evil things going on around us.

(3) God expects leaders to treat people fairly, eliminate evil practices, and to live a life that is pleasing to Him.

HANDPICKED TO SERVE

#WhatIlearned:

_____

_____

_____

_____

_____

_____

A GOOD LEADER KNOWS...

That they're already equipped for the job

You can do it!

Lesson Text: Exodus 4: 10-17

¹⁰ But Moses pleaded with the LORD, "O Lord, I'm not very good with words. I never have been, and I'm not now, even though you have spoken to me. I get tongue-tied, and my words get tangled."

¹¹ Then the LORD asked Moses, "Who makes a person's mouth? Who decides whether people speak or do not speak, hear or do not hear, see or do not see? Is it not I, the LORD? ¹² Now go! I will be with you as you speak, and I will instruct you in what to say." ¹³ But Moses again pleaded, "Lord, please! Send anyone else."

¹⁴ Then the LORD became angry with Moses. "All right," he said. "What about your brother, Aaron the Levite? I know he speaks well. And look! He is on his way to meet you now. He will be delighted to see you.¹⁵ Talk to him, and put the words in his mouth. I will be with both of you as you speak, and I will instruct you both in what to do. ¹⁶ Aaron will be your spokesman to the people. He will be your mouthpiece, and you will stand in the place of God for him, telling him what to say.

¹⁷ And take your shepherd's staff with you, and use it to perform the miraculous signs I have shown you."

P2P Then:

- Before he fled for the dessert, Moses was educated in the best schools in Egypt, and was mighty in words and deeds (Acts 7:22). So, he was already equipped for the task that God had assigned to him.

- God had Moses take the things that he already had, to use as signs that God was with him. He had him use his rod, his hand, his voice, and even his brother. (Exodus 4: 1-9)

- Although Moses had gained the skills necessary to free and lead the Israelites to the Promised Land, he still felt inadequate for the task. He was looking for reasons and excuses to get out of the assignment, but God reminded Moses that He would teach Moses what to say and do when the time came.

_____

_____

P2P Now:

- God takes joy in using ordinary things (our abilities and talents) for extraordinary purposes. We have to be confident and aware of those things that makes us unique.

- Some people have some extraordinary talents and abilities that seem to make our gifts look small. We have to remember that our talents are just as important, and we can make everyday contributions.

- Although we may feel inadequate for the things that God will have us to do, if we just look back at our past, we will see that God was teaching, training and equipping us for what will come in our lives.

_____

_____

Real Talk:

Have you ever felt like someone was better than you and that they should be the leader or do the task instead of you?

Life Lessons:

(1) Some of the things that we go through are really helping us prepare for the future.

(2) We are all unique and should not belittle the talents and abilities that God has blessed us with.

(3) We can't always focus on our weaknesses or let feelings of inadequacy and fear keep us from going forward.

(4) We have to appreciate and learn how to use our gifts to accomplish the task.

#WhatIlearned:

_____

_____

_____

_____

_____

_____

_____

www.ingramcontent.com/pod-product-compliance
Lightning Source LLC
Chambersburg PA
CBHW070552300426
44113CB00011B/1884